It's Your Turn Snoopy

Charles M. Schulz

CORONET BOOKS
Hodder Fawcett, London

Copyright © 1972, 1973 by
United Feature Syndicate Inc.

First published by Fawcett Publications Inc.,
New York

Coronet edition 1978
Eighth impression 1981

Printed and bound in Great Britain for Hodder
Fawcett Ltd., Mill Road, Dunton Green,
Sevenoaks, Kent (Editorial Office:
47 Bedford Square, London, WC1 3DP) by
Cox & Wyman Ltd., Reading

ISBN 0 340 22778 8

It's your turn, SNOOPY

HELLO, PEPPERMINT PATTY? WE'RE THINKING ABOUT HAVING A TESTIMONIAL DINNER FOR CHARLIE BROWN... COULD YOU COME?

WHAT HAPPENS AT A TESTIMONIAL DINNER?

WELL, EVERYONE GETS UP, AND SAYS ALL SORTS OF THINGS ABOUT WHAT A GREAT PERSON THE GUEST OF HONOR IS...

IT'S GOING TO BE A QUIET EVENING!

Dear Joe Shlabotnik, How would you like to be our Master of Ceremonies?

We are having a testimonial dinner for our manager who is also your number-one fan.

WON'T IT BE GREAT IF HE CAN COME? JOE SHLABOTNIK IS CHARLIE BROWN'S FAVORITE BASEBALL PLAYER..

HE PROBABLY WON'T BE ABLE TO GET AWAY... THEY'RE PRETTY BUSY DOWN AT THE CAR WASH!

LOOK! I RECEIVED AN ANSWER FROM JOE SHLABOTNIK!

"DEAR FRIENDS, I ACCEPT YOUR INVITATION TO ATTEND THE TESTIMONIAL DINNER FOR MR. BROWN.. MY USUAL FEE FOR SUCH AFFAIRS IS ONE HUNDRED DOLLARS"

ONE HUNDRED DOLLARS?!! TELL HIM THAT ALL WE CAN AFFORD IS FIFTY CENTS..

"P.S. I'LL TAKE IT!"

HOW ARE PLANS GOING FOR THE BIG TESTIMONIAL DINNER, LINUS?

GREAT! HAVE YOU EVER HEARD OF JOE SHLABOTNIK? HE WAS LAST-ROUND DRAFT CHOICE IN THE GREEN GRASS LEAGUE...

HE'S GOING TO BE OUR GUEST SPEAKER

HOW APPROPRIATE!

OKAY, MARCIE, YOU AND I ARE THE INVITATION COMMITTEE

NOW, HERE'S A LIST OF ALL THE PEOPLE WHO ARE TO RECEIVE INVITATIONS TO CHARLIE BROWN'S TESTIMONIAL DINNER .... AT THE BOTTOM OF EACH ONE, WE PUT R.S.V.P.

WHAT DOES R.S.V.P. MEAN, SIR?

"REVISED STANDARD VERSION, PLEASE"

I NEVER UNDERSTAND YOUR JOKES, SIR...

STOP CALLING ME "SIR"!

HELLO, CHUCK? AS CHAIRWOMAN OF THE INVITATION COMMITTEE, I HAVE A SURPRISE FOR YOU!

I COULDN'T TELL YOU BEFORE BECAUSE THIS HAS ALL BEEN VERY HUSH-HUSH, BUT NOW I CAN TELL YOU...GUESS WHAT...WE'RE GOING TO GIVE YOU A TESTIMONIAL DINNER!!

HOW DOES THAT HIT YOU, CHUCK? ARE YOU EXCITED? ARE YOU SMILING, CHUCK?

I'M SMILING!!!

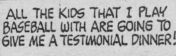

WHO IN THE WORLD COULD BE CALLING AT THREE O'CLOCK IN THE MORNING?

WHO? NO, THE DINNER WAS CANCELED...WELL, IT'S A LONG STORY...

YES, WE WERE WONDERING WHAT HAD HAPPENED TO YOU...I'M SORRY YOU GOT LOST...ALL RIGHT...MAYBE NEXT TIME...

GOOD NIGHT, MR. SHLABOTNIK

"A PINCH-HITTER MAY BE DESIGNATED TO BAT FOR THE STARTING PITCHER AND ALL SUBSEQUENT PITCHERS IN ANY GAME WITHOUT OTHERWISE AFFECTING THE STATUS OF THE PITCHERS IN THE GAME.."

" FAILURE TO DESIGNATE A PINCH-HITTER PRIOR TO THE GAME PRECLUDES THE USE OF A DESIGNATED PINCH-HITTER FOR THE GAME... PINCH-HITTERS FOR A DESIGNATED PINCH-HITTER MAY BE USED..."

"ANY SUBSTITUTE PINCH-HITTER FOR A DESIGNATED PINCH-HITTER HIMSELF BECOMES A DESIGNATED PINCH-HITTER..A REPLACED DESIGNATED PINCH-HITTER SHALL NOT RE-ENTER THE GAME"

I . PROBABLY WON'T GET TO BAT THE WHOLE SEASON...

SCHULZ

Dear Dog, This is to inform you that you are one of the finalists for this year's Daisy Hill Puppy Cup Award.

THE DAISY HILL PUPPY CUP!! I'VE BEEN NOMINATED FOR THE DAISY HILL PUPPY CUP!!!

WHEEEEEE!

STUPID BEAGLE!

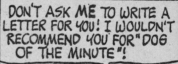

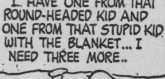

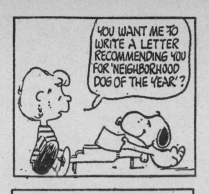

WHEN YOU'VE LOST AT SOMETHING, YOU CAN REACT IN TWO WAYS...

ONE WAY IS TO ANALYZE JUST WHY YOU LOST...TRY TO FIGURE OUT WHAT YOUR WEAKNESSES WERE, AND THEN TRY TO IMPROVE SO THAT NEXT TIME YOU CAN WIN...

BLEAH!

THAT'S THE OTHER WAY!

→

YOU JUST THINK YOU'RE CUTE BECAUSE YOU'RE CUTE!

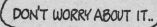

I KNEW THIS WAS GOING TO HAPPEN SOMETIME...

MY BLANKET HAS BEEN RECALLED!

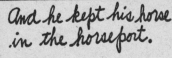

A NEW MONTH AGAIN..

TODAY IS APRIL FOOL'S DAY, CHARLIE BROWN..

I THINK I'LL PLAY A LITTLE JOKE ON YOU...I THINK I'LL TRY A LITTLE TRICK...

YOU UNDERSTAND WHAT I'M SAYING, DON'T YOU? YOU UNDERSTAND THAT THIS IS APRIL FOOL'S DAY? YOU'RE SURE? I WANT TO BE CERTAIN THAT YOU UNDERSTAND! OKAY?

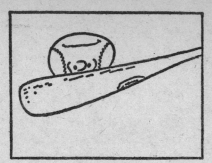

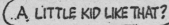

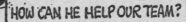

WE WON, CHARLIE BROWN! C'MON, LET'S GO HOME, AND CELEBRATE!

NO! FIRST I HAVE TO WAIT FOR THE OPPOSING MANAGER TO COME OVER AND CONGRATULATE ME

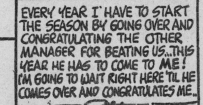

EVERY YEAR I HAVE TO START THE SEASON BY GOING OVER AND CONGRATULATING THE OTHER MANAGER FOR BEATING US...THIS YEAR HE HAS TO COME TO ME! I'M GOING TO WAIT RIGHT HERE 'TIL HE COMES OVER AND CONGRATULATES ME..

HEY, BIG BROTHER, THE TELEPHONE WAS FOR YOU

BUT I JUST GOT TO SLEEP...

IT WAS SOME MAN WITH A DEEP VOICE

I THINK HE SAID HE WAS THE LEAGUE PRESIDENT

THE LEAGUE PRESIDENT? WHY WOULD HE BE CALLING ME?

HEY! THE PHONE ISN'T EVEN OFF THE HOOK!

I HUNG UP ON HIM!!

RERUN, YOU REALLY LET ME DOWN!

I WAS THE ONE WHO TALKED CHARLIE BROWN INTO LETTING YOU PLAY; SO THEN YOU GO AND GET US INVOLVED IN A BETTING SCANDAL!

I ONLY BET A NICKEL...WHAT ELSE CAN YOU DO WITH A NICKEL THESE DAYS?

OF COURSE, I MUST ADMIT ONE THING...

YOU'RE THE FIRST PERSON WHO EVER HAD THE COURAGE TO BET ON CHARLIE BROWN'S TEAM

I'LL DRINK TO THAT!

HE'S COMING! HE'S COMING!

THANK YOU, EASTER BEAGLE! THANK YOU!

THANK YOU

THANK YOU VERY MUCH

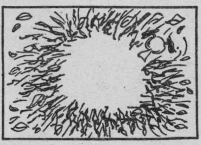

ACTUALLY, WOODSTOCK PROBABLY SHOULDN'T HAVE A PAPER DELIVERED TO HIS HOME..

WOODSTOCK WOULD HAVE MADE A LOUSY MOTH!

FOR THE LOVE OF PEANUTS

All these books are available at your local bookshop or newsagent, or can be ordered direct from the publisher. Just tick the titles you want and fill in the form below.

Prices and availability subject to change without notice.

CORONET BOOKS, P.O. Box 11, Falmouth, Cornwall.

Please send cheque or postal order, and allow the following for postage and packing:

U.K. — 40p for one book, plus 18p for the second book, and 13p for each additional book ordered up to a £1.49 maximum.

B.F.P.O. and EIRE — 40p for the first book, plus 18p for the second book, and 13p per copy for the next 7 books, 7p per book thereafter.

OTHER OVERSEAS CUSTOMERS — 60p for the first book, plus 18p per copy for each additional book.

Name ....

Address..

....